KELLY CLARKSON

Her Journey from Idol to Icon

Leona A. Handy

TABLE OF CONTENTS

CHAPTER 1 INTRODUCTION

Kelly Clarkson is an American vocalist, songwriter, and television personality. She soared to popularity in 2002 after bringing home the American Idol trophy and inking a record contract with RCA. "A Moment Like This", her maiden success, gained the top place on the US Billboard Hot 100 and ended up being the best-selling song in that nation in 2002. The song was featured on her first studio album, Thankful, which was released in 2003 and debuted at the top of the Billboard 200.

Since then, Clarkson has produced nine studio albums, each of which has garnered financial success. She has also received a lot of prizes, including three Grammy prizes, four American Music Awards, and two Academy of Country Music Awards. She is the first performer in music history to simultaneously top the pop, adult contemporary, adult pop, country, and dance charts.

In addition to coaching The Voice from its fourteenth season through its twenty-first season, and once more for its twenty-third season, Clarkson has a successful singing career. Since 2019, she has served as the host of her own talk show, The Kelly Clarkson program.

Clarkson's comments and commanding voice are well-known. She is a role model for many young girls and regularly receives praise for her candor and genuineness. She is a fierce advocate for spreading awareness of mental health concerns and has openly shared her struggles with anxiety and hopelessness.

Clarkson is a well-known and skilled performer who has impacted the music industry. She is an inspiration to many people and will undoubtedly continue to amuse and inspire people for a very long time.

Here are some more details about Kelly Clarkson:

- Her three children are River Rose, Remington Alexander, and Remy Anne.
- She was married to Brandon Blackstock.
- Although she has stated in interviews that she is not a fundamentalist when it comes to her beliefs, she has a strong trust in Christ.
- The American Red Cross, St. Jude Children's Research Hospital, and the Humane Society of the United States are just a few of the organizations she has worked with and shows she is giving-spirited.

CHAPTER 2 EARLY LIFE

Kelly Clarkson was born on April 24, 1982, in Fort Worth, Texas. She is the youngest of three children, with a brother called Jason and a sister named Alyssa. Jeanne and Stephen Clarkson separated when the young girl was six years old. Later, Clarkson's mother got remarried to Jimmy Taylor.

Burleson, Texas, a suburb of Fort Worth, is where Clarkson was reared. She attended Pauline Hughes Middle School and Burleson High School. In the seventh grade, Cynthia Glenn, the choir teacher at the school, saw her singing in a hallway and urged her to try out for the chorus. According to Clarkson, she never had any formal voice lessons.

Clarkson continued to participate in the school chorus throughout her time in high school. She also had appearances in musicals including Annie Get Your Gun, Brigadoon, and Seven Brides for Seven Brothers. After graduating from high school in 2000, Clarkson worked as a pharmacy clerk and waiter at a comedy club.

Clarkson auditioned for the 2002 season of American Idol. She quickly gained popularity and eventually took the title. "A Moment Like This," her debut hit, reached the top spot on the US Billboard Hot 100 and ended up becoming the best-selling single in that country in 2002. The song was included on her debut studio album, Thankful, which was released in 2003 and debuted at the top of the Billboard 200.

The rest, as they say, is history. After then, Clarkson recorded nine studio albums, all of which were commercially successful. She has also won a number of awards, including three Grammy Awards, four American Music Awards, and two Academy of Country Music Awards. She is the only artist in music history to concurrently top the pop, adult contemporary, adult pop, country, and dance charts.

In addition to coaching The Voice from its fourteenth season through its twenty-first season, and once more for its twenty-third season, Clarkson has a successful singing career. Since 2019, she has served as the host of her own talk show, The Kelly Clarkson program.

2.1 Career Beginnings

Kelly Clarkson's career officially began when she auditioned for American Idol's inaugural season in 2002.

She was 20 years old at the time and had never been inside a recording studio before. Her charisma and amazing voice, however, won over the judges and the audience right away. She ultimately won the competition, making history as the first American Idol champion.

After winning American Idol, Clarkson agreed to a recording contract with RCA Records. Her debut single, "A Moment Like This," which debuted at the top of the Billboard Hot 100 list, was the best-selling song in the country in 2002. The song was included on her debut studio album, Thankful, which was released in 2003 and debuted at the top of the Billboard 200.

The book Thankful was a commercial and critical success in the US, selling over 12 million copies. The Top 10 hits "Low" and "Miss Independent" were born from it. Clarkson's fame increased after the release of her second album, Breakaway (2004), which garnered over 12 million sales in the US and a Grammy Award for Best Pop Vocal Album.

Clarkson has released nine studio albums since winning American Idol, and each one of them has achieved commercial success. She has also appeared in a number of films, including From Justin to Kelly (2003) and The Princess Diaries 2: Royal Engagement (2004).

2.2 American Idol

Kelly Clarkson's journey on American Idol was nothing short of extraordinary. At the age of 20, she started working as a waitress in Texas with the goal of becoming a singer. She quickly won over the hearts of the public as well as the judges because of her appealing personality and powerful voice.

Clarkson reached the championship round and competed against Justin Guarini there. In the end, Clarkson was crowned the winner of American Idol's first season. Additionally, she won a $1 million award and signed a recording contract with RCA Records.

After winning American Idol, Clarkson gained widespread recognition. Since its 2003 release, Thankful, her self-titled first album, has sold more than 12 million copies in the US. She has released nine additional albums since then, all of which have done well in the market. In addition, Clarkson has received 16 other Grammy nominations and three Grammy Awards.

Clarkson has appeared in a variety of films and TV episodes in addition to her musical endeavors. She has additionally worked with singers competing on the TV show The Voice.

Clarkson is among the best vocalists of all time. Her records have sold more than 50 million copies worldwide, and she has won several awards. Her life is a tribute to the power of dreams, and she is an inspiration to countless numbers of people throughout the globe.

A couple of Kelly Clarkson's American Idol accomplishments are listed below:

- She went to the St. Louis, Missouri, casting call for the program.
- She sang "At Last" at her audition.
- Throughout the whole competition, she held the lead.
- She sang a duet with Reba McEntire.
- She sang "A Moment Like This," which peaked at number one, at the show's climax.
- She triumphed in the contest on September 4, 2002.

The American Idol story of Kelly Clarkson is one of fantasies coming true. She is an inspiration to millions of people across the world, and her tale proves that everything is possible if you set your mind to it.

CHAPTER 3 PERSONAL LIFE

Clarkson is divorced from Brandon Blackstock, the son of her former manager Narvel Blackstock, and former stepson of country icon Reba McEntire. The duo married in 2013 and have two children together, River Rose and Remington Alexander. In 2022, they got divorced.

Since she is currently unmarried, Clarkson has stated that she has no plans to date or remarry anytime soon. Her priorities are her family and her singing career.

A more thorough summary of Kelly Clarkson's private life may be found here:

- Jeanne Ann (née Rose) and Stephen Michael Clarkson are the parents.
- Alyssa and Jason are siblings.
- Brandon Blackstock, an ex-husband (married 2013, divorced in 2022).
- River Rose was born in 2014, and Remington Alexander was born in 2016.
- Relationship status right now: single

Being a reserved individual, Clarkson rarely discusses her personal life in public. In a few interviews, she has raised the subject of her divorce from Blackstock. Although she has admitted that it was a bad time for her, she is now in a better place. Kelly Clarkson and Brandon Blackstock were wed for over seven years before filing for divorce in June 2020. She is currently focused on her singing business and her children, and she has no immediate plans to date or remarry.

3.1 Marriage and Divorce

While Clarkson was still in the beginning stages of her career, Blackstock and Clarkson first crossed paths in 2006. Blackstock was representing Clarkson's former manager, Narvel Blackstock, who was working as a talent manager at the time. They started dating in 2011, and in December 2012, they got engaged. In a secret ceremony in Tennessee, they were united in marriage in October 2013.

Using the grounds of "irreconcilable differences," Clarkson filed for divorce from Blackstock in June 2020. She wanted primary physical custody of their children as well as spousal maintenance and child support payments from Blackstock. In a counter-petition for divorce, Blackstock once more cited "irreconcilable differences."

Both sides allegedly accused the other of infidelity and financial misdeeds throughout the divorce proceedings, which were reportedly contentious. A judge awarded Clarkson a preliminary injunction against Blackstock in September 2021, preventing him from selling the Montana property the two co-owned. In March 2022, the divorce was finally finalized.

In interviews, Clarkson has been open about her divorce, saying that while it was a difficult time for her, she is now in a better place. She has said that she is concentrating on her singing profession and her kids, and that she is not planning on dating or remarrying anytime soon.

He has now begun dating actress Rena Sofer. Blackstock has also commented on the divorce, calling it "heartbreaking" but asserting that he is "moving on."

It was widely reported that Kelly Clarkson and Brandon Blackstock's divorce was a high-profile split. It serves as a reminder that even happy marriages may break down. But Clarkson's ability to put the divorce behind her and concentrate on her career and children is also a testament to her fortitude and fortitude.

3.2 Children

With her ex-husband Brandon Blackstock, Kelly
Clarkson has two kids: River Rose was born in 2014,
and Remington Alexander was born in 2016.

River Rose is a bubbly, outgoing child who enjoys
singing and dancing. She likes learning new things and is
highly brilliant. Remington Alexander, who is more
quiet, likes to play with cars and trucks. He also likes to
cuddle and is quite loving.

Clarkson says she is immensely grateful to be their
mother and that her kids are "everything" to her. She has
also said that she hopes to instill in her children a sense
of independence, empathy, and kindness.

Below is some information on Clarkson's kids:

- River Rose is the name of the river that runs
  through Clarkson's hometown of Burleson,
  Texas.
- Remington Alexander was given its name in
  honor of Clarkson's grandfather, a pilot.
- The children are bilingual in English and
  Spanish.

- Clarkson says she is immensely grateful to be their mother and that her kids are "everything" to her.

Clarkson routinely shares pictures and videos of her children on social media as a devoted mother. She is very open about the challenges of parenting, such as the time she had to take River Rose to the hospital due to an allergic reaction.

Because Clarkson provides an example of how it is possible to have both a rewarding career and a dedicated family, many parents find inspiration in her.

3.3 Her Parenting Philosophies

According to Kelly Clarkson, she adopts a lenient and assertive parenting approach. She firmly believes in laying out standards and expectations for her kids, but she also wants them to know that she is proud of them and is there for them. Although she has stated that she is not afraid to discipline her children harshly when required, she also wants them to know that they can confide in her about everything.

Kelly Clarkson has the following parenting philosophies:

- She favors clearly defining expectations and regulations. Clarkson is not hesitant to enforce the rules because she wants her kids to understand what is expected of them. She has stated that while she occasionally believes in "tough love," she also wants her children to know that she is there for them.
- She aspires for her kids to be self-sufficient. Clarkson wants her kids to develop independence and the capacity for self-decision-making. In addition to providing them with the resources they need to thrive in life, she has stated that she also wants them to know that she is always available to them.
- She wants her children to have compassion and kindness. Clarkson wants her kids to have empathy and kindness towards others. She has stated that she wants them to have the ability to speak up for what they are passionate about and to provide a hand to those in need.
- She wants her kids to be content. Raising contented kids is Clarkson's first priority as a parent. She has stated that she wants them to enjoy a happy, joyful, and adventurous childhood.

Kelly Clarkson is a caring mother who is determined to give her kids a healthy and encouraging atmosphere to grow up in. She believes in establishing clear standards and expectations while still showing love and support, and her parenting style is a blend of the authoritarian and indulgent. She hopes for autonomous, good-natured, caring, and contented children.

3.4 Philanthropy

Kelly Clarkson, a well-known singer, songwriter, and television personality, is also well-known for her charity. She has contributed to several charitable causes and groups throughout the years, including:

- The Kelly Clarkson Fund: In 2012, Kelly Clarkson founded the nonprofit organization of the same name. The fund supports a multitude of programs, including adoption, foster care, and animal welfare.
- Musicians on Call: This ensemble provides live music for patients in hospitals and other healthcare facilities. Clarkson has long been a vocal supporter of Musicians on Call and has even performed at their events.
- Children's Miracle Network Hospitals: This organization raises money for children's hospitals around the nation. Children's Miracle Network

Hospitals has used Clarkson as a spokesperson since 2010, and she has even performed at telethons for the charity.

- Feeding America is the largest hunger relief organization in the nation. Clarkson has partnered with Feeding America to help end hunger and facilitate the provision of meals to those in need.
- The Trevor Project provides crisis intervention and suicide prevention services for LGBTQ+ youth. Clarkson has long been a supporter of The Trevor Project and has even given a performance at one of their galas.

In addition, Clarkson has used her influence to promote important topics including mental health and body acceptance . She serves as an inspiration to many, and her humanitarian efforts are transforming the world.

In addition to the organizations already listed, Clarkson has supported a broad range of additional causes, such as:

- Clarkson has donated blood to the American Red Cross and has invited her fans to do the same.
- The Make-A-Wish Foundation: Clarkson has granted the wishes of several Make-A-Wish children.

- In addition to providing financial contributions, Clarkson has supported the Humane Society of the United States by adopting animals from its facilities. She cherishes animals.

3.5 Weight Loss Journey

Kelly Clarkson followed the Plant Paradox diet, which excludes lectins, and shed 37 pounds in 2018. Lectins, a kind of protein present in various plant foods, have been linked to weight gain and inflammation in some individuals. Lectin-containing foods including grains, beans, nightshade vegetables, and dairy products are avoided on the Plant Paradox diet.

Clarkson modified her lifestyle in addition to adhering to the Plant Paradox diet. She started receiving more frequent exercise and rest. She also meditated and did yoga to lower her stress levels.

In addition to encouraging people to choose a diet and way of life that works for them, Clarkson has been transparent about her own weight reduction struggle. She has stated that she is working to improve her health and weight for herself, not for anyone else.

Here is a more thorough examination of Kelly Clarkson's weight loss process:

- What motivated her to become in shape? Clarkson said that after reading Dr. Steven Gundry's book The Plant Paradox, she was motivated to start a weight-loss program. The book makes the case that lectins can contribute to inflammation and weight gain and that a lectin-free diet can aid in weight loss and health enhancement.
- Which diet did she adhere to? The Plant Paradox diet, which excludes lectins, was followed by Clarkson. This indicates that she cut out lectin-containing foods including grains, legumes, nightshade vegetables, and dairy goods.
- Which workout did she perform? Clarkson began working out more frequently, concentrating on both cardio and weight training. In order to lessen tension, she also started attending yoga and meditation sessions.
- How much did she decrease in weight? In 2018, Clarkson dropped 37 pounds. Although she has stated that she still wants to reduce a few more pounds, she is content with her current progress.

Many people who are attempting to get healthier and reduce weight find motivation in Kelly Clarkson. She is living proof that you may reduce your weight in a healthy way without giving up the meals you enjoy.

CHAPTER 4 DISCOGRAPHY

Kelly Clarkson has released 10 studio albums, 7 extended plays, 1 compilation album, 1 remix album, and 10 singles in addition to 55 singles (including 8 as a featured artist). Additionally, she offers a selection of live CDs and DVDs.

The following is a list of her studio albums, along with their release dates, some of their biggest hits, and other information:

- Clarkson's debut album, Thankful (2003), produced the songs "A Moment Like This," "Miss Independent," and "Low."
- The critically praised and commercially successful album Breakaway (2004) is the source of the popular songs "Breakaway," "Because of You," and "Since U Been Gone."
- On her more personal album, My December (2007), Clarkson looked into topics like melancholy and loss. Three of the album's songs have been released as singles: "Never Again," "Don't Waste Your Time," and "One Minute."

- On Clarkson's 2009 album All I Ever Wanted, which saw a return to her more pop-oriented sound, the hit songs "My Life Would Suck Without You," "I Do Not Hook Up," and "Stronger" were all included.
- Stronger, Clarkson's 2011 album, has a more electronic vibe than her past albums. The album's hits include "Mr. Know It All," "What Doesn't Kill You (Stronger)," and "Dark Side."
- Clarkson's debut Christmas album, Wrapped in Red (2013), has the top-charting singles "Wrapped in Red" and "Underneath the Tree."
- The inspiration for the 2015 album Piece by Piece, which examines themes of tenacity and perseverance, came from Clarkson and Brandon Blackstock's divorce. The album's three hits were "Heartbeat Song," "Piece by Piece," and "Invincible."
- The chart-topping singles "Love So Soft," "Move You," and "I Don't Think About You" from Clarkson's 2017 album Meaning of Life signaled a return to her more pop-oriented sound.
- As the holidays approach... This is Clarkson's second holiday album, which included the number-one singles "Christmas Isn't Canceled (Just You)" and "December."

- Chemistry (2023): This is Clarkson's ninth studio album, which has the number-one singles "Mine" and "Me."

Additionally, Clarkson has made a number of live CDs and DVDs accessible, including:

- During the Breakaway tour, Kelly Clarkson recorded the live CD Kelly Clarkson: Live in Concert (2004).
- Kelly Clarkson: All I Ever Wanted: Live in Manila (2010): During the All I Ever Wanted tour, this live CD was recorded in Manila, Philippines.
- Piece by Piece: Live, Kelly Clarkson's 2016 live album, was captured when the singer was on tour to promote the album.
- Kelly Clarkson recorded this live CD while on the Meaning of Life World Tour in 2018.

Clarkson, a singer, has enjoyed both critical and financial success. She has received 16 additional Grammy Award nominations, and she has taken home three of them. She has also won a Daytime Emmy Award for her talk show, The Kelly Clarkson Show.

Clarkson is one of the most well-known vocalists in the world. She has sold more than 100 million singles and more than 50 million albums worldwide. She is an inspiration for young girls everywhere and a motivator for many people.

CHAPTER 5 AWARDS AND NOMINATIONS

Kelly Clarkson is a Grammy-winning singer, songwriter, television personality, and award winner. She has been nominated for and won several accolades throughout the course of her career, including:

- Triple Grammys : Three Grammy Awards have been given to Clarkson for her album Breakaway from 2006, Best Pop Vocal Album, Best Pop Solo Performance (for "Stronger" in 2012), and Best Country Duo/Group Performance (for "Don't You Wanna Stay" with Jason Aldean in 2013).

- 4 American Music Awards: For Artist of the Year, Favorite Pop/Rock Female Artist, and Favorite Adult Contemporary Artist, respectively, Clarkson received four American Music Awards in 2005, 2006, and 2012.

- 2 Academy of Country Music Awards: Clarkson has won two Academy of Country Music Awards, for her duet with Jason Aldean on "Don't

You Wanna Stay" in 2013 and for Top New Female Vocalist in 2006.

- 5 Daytime Emmy Awards: Kelly Clarkson won five Daytime Emmy Awards for Outstanding Entertainment Talk Show Host and Outstanding Talk Show Entertainment for her work on The Kelly Clarkson Show in the years 2020, 2021, and 2022.

- One MTV Video Music Award: In 2005, "Since U Been Gone" won Clarkson the MTV Video Music Award for Best Female Video.

Clarkson has also been nominated for a number of additional awards, such as:

- The Grammys, sixteen
- 11 American Music Awards
- There are six Academy of Country Music awards.
- 12 winners of the People's Choice Award
- eleventh Billboard Music Awards

Clarkson is a highly regarded musician, and her nominations and awards attest to her talent and success. She is still one of the most well-known and successful singers in the world, and many people look up to her.

CHAPTER 6 LEGACY AND IMPACT

In her career as a singer, songwriter, and television personality, Kelly Clarkson has achieved enormous success. Nine of her studio albums have been commercial successes since she was the first American Idol winner. Clarkson has also won four American Music Awards, three Grammy Awards, five Daytime Emmy Awards, two Academy of Country Music Awards, four American Music Awards, and one MTV Video Music Award. She is a well-known television personality who has been hosting her own talk show, The Kelly Clarkson Show, since 2019.

Clarkson's lyrics and commanding voice are well-known. She has composed songs about a variety of topics, including love, grief, empowerment, and self-discovery. Millions of people all across the world have been inspired and motivated by her songs.

Among Clarkson's charitable initiatives are The Kelly Clarkson Fund, Musicians on Call, Children's Miracle

Network Hospitals, Feeding America, and The Trevor Project. She is also a generous giver. Many people find inspiration in her, and her work is altering the course of history.

Sincere icon Clarkson will continue to have a lasting impact for many years to come. She acts as a role model for young girls all around the world by showing them that it is possible to have both a rewarding career and a loving family life. She also uses her platform to raise awareness about important issues like LGBTQ+ rights, body acceptance, and mental health. She is an outspoken supporter of social justice.

The significance of Kelly Clarkson's legacy and her singularity are explained in different ways as follows:

- She is a talented singer and composer with a powerful voice.
- She is authentic and personable.
- She is admired by many individuals, especially young women.
- She is a humanitarian who uses her position to better the world.
- She is a wonderful example of body positivity and accepting oneself.
- She is a vocal advocate for social justice.

Kelly Clarkson is a true icon, and she will continue to have a lasting impact for many years to come.

Made in the USA
Middletown, DE
16 December 2023

45723705R00018